SAGITTARIUS
November 22–December 21

Crystal Astrology for Modern Life

SANDY SITRON

CONTENTS

CRYSTALS, ASTROLOGY AND YOU

UNDERSTANDING SAGITTARIUS

CRYSTALS, ASTROLOGY AND YOU

THE STONES,
THE SIGNS AND YOU

The stars above you and the stones beneath your feet are part of the fabric of your world. Astrology offers a cosmic perspective. Crystals radiate with the healing energy of the Earth. Together, they serve as guides in your life, engaged in a vibrational conversation that can help you reflect on, and tune into, who you are. Birthstones and other crystals can be used to highlight and harness the energy of your astrological birth chart.

As above, so below – harness the power of crystals and the cosmos to create a deeper connection with yourself for a confident, empowered, high-vibe life.

Astrology is the ancient study of the changing positions and alternating energy of the celestial bodies and how this relates to our lives on Earth. The unique cosmic environment that you synced up with at the moment of your first breath provides awareness of – and offers a way to interpret – your personality traits, core strengths, growth areas, emotional style and so much more. When you better understand your vibrational self, it's easier to make informed choices about the big and small things in your life. Your conscious perspective is uplifted. Your mind is opened and activated.

Crystals, or 'stones', vibrate with the breath of the Earth. They act on an energetic level, sending vibrations out into the world. They are natural amplifiers of positive energy and bring discordant energies into balance. Each crystal has its own energy blueprint, which is why different types of stones may influence the human energy field in different ways. Pairing the insight that you gain from astrology with the healing power of crystals can help you navigate certain life areas and facilitate personal transformation and spiritual growth throughout the astrological year.

Crystals and the constellations call to us. In this book you'll receive a bespoke selection of crystals to help you amplify or balance the unique energies of your sign. You'll gain insight into your life, activate your highest potential and learn to live harmoniously with the energy that surrounds you.

When gazing at the night sky, when you hold a crystal in your hand, feel inspired to slow down, be present in the moment and get ready to embark on a meaningful journey of self-discovery.

YOUR UNIQUE RECOMMENDATIONS

We all accept that different things work for different people. Advice that's a perfect fit for one person might fall flat for someone else. Regardless of where Sagittarius sits in your personal astrology, this book will help you understand your Sagittarius nature and give you specific crystal recommendations for your sign and each astrological season. You can use these bespoke Sagittarius crystals to build confidence, spark creativity, feel more present, harmonize relationships, attract love, embrace your emotions, cultivate friendships, create abundance, optimize your health and wellness, amplify your natural gifts and find balance.

YOUR ASTRO-CRYSTAL JOURNEY

Once you understand how the two energetic studies of crystals and astrology relate to your life, you'll be ready to take a deep dive into your Sagittarius energy and learn to use crystals to leverage the strengths of your Sagittarius gifts, whether Sagittarius is your Sun, Moon or Rising sign, or elsewhere in your unique astrology. You'll also discover your unique Sagittarius crystal recommendations for love, friendship, money, work and health to help you connect to your true potential and reach your dreams and goals.

As each astrological season holds a different kind of energy, this book will take you through the year and show you how crystals can help you channel your unique Sagittarius energy under each sign. In this way, you will learn to navigate through the seasons with ease and to harmonize with the cycles of nature. You will discover how crystals can help you embrace the ebb and flow of the 29-day Moon cycle, enable you to sail through Mercury Retrograde and even plan your week.

This book is part of a series that unites each of the twelve zodiac signs with recommended crystals. When you are ready to go deeper on your astro-crystal journey, you may choose to purchase the companion books in the series that correspond to the other prominent signs in your birth chart.

THE STONES

Dazzling gemstones are typically formed deep under the Earth's surface, stimulated by the combination of mineral-rich water, heat and pressure. Subterranean 'gardens' nurture the formation of billions of atoms into highly ordered, three-dimensional repeating patterns to create unique crystals, each one holding a vibrational record of earthly, physical reality.

Across the world and over millennia, people have been fascinated by crystals. Lucent jewels have captured the imagination for over 30,000 years. In the Democratic Republic of the Congo, small tools decorated with Quartz have been found that date back to 33,000 BCE. The Ancient Sumerians of Mesopotamia (present-day Iraq) used crystals for rituals and magic in the fourth century BCE. Humankind has used crystals for decoration, status, currency, religion, healing, magic-making and, in more recent times, modern technology. Early radios used crystals as electrical and tuning components. Today's computers, LCD screens and some batteries rely on crystal technology.

Good Vibrations   People across different cultures and generations have turned to crystals as guides or helpers because it seems that, whatever facet of earthly experience you are struggling with, there is a crystal frequency that can help you move forwards on your path. Crystals may help bring calm and heal stress, empower you when you need support or confidence, or provide focus and clarity when you're struggling with an important decision. Crystals are thought to absorb the energy that you are trying to release and release the energy you are trying to absorb.

For example, if you are feeling dull and listless, Carnelian may share with you a vibration of high energy and drive. If you are overheated or stressed, Rose Quartz may help you soften and relax. Choosing the right crystal that resonates with, or reacts to, your energy can shift your mood or your mindset.

CHOOSING YOUR CRYSTALS

In Part Two of this book, you will be guided to a selection of crystals that are energetically aligned with your unique astrology. If you are adding these stones to your collection, it's important to choose responsibly.

Sustainability and Ethics   How did the crystal that you have in your hand make its way to you? The answer to this question is incredibly important to the well-being of humanity and the Earth.

The crystal industry is shrouded in mystery and plagued by bad practices. When you purchase a crystal, make sure to find gems that have a traceable, and short, journey from the mine to your hand. It's important to know if the mine that the crystal came from uses ethical, safe and sustainable practices. Discover if the lapidary, where the crystal was cut and polished, is a safe place that pays a living wage to the people who work there. The easiest way to do this is to mindfully source your crystals from sellers who have done the legwork. You vote with your financial choices. Make sure that you are contributing to better health and safety for all.

More information about sustainable and ethical practices and purveyors can be found on my website www.sandysitron.com/crystals.

Size, Finish and Price   When harnessing the power of a crystal for personal use, the size of the stone doesn't matter. If you are holding a crystal or carrying it close to your body, its vibration is in your energy field and will have an effect whatever its size.

A raw stone is a stone that is untreated. These are just as effective to use in healing practices as a crystal that has been tumbled or polished. So when you are choosing a crystal, choose one that appeals to you, no matter the size or finish.

The stones selected in this book can be sourced at an affordable price. Although some of the stones mentioned may sound ultra-luxurious and expensive, these crystals are available at a range of values.

YOUR CRYSTAL TOOLKIT

In the next section, you'll find crystal recommendations for your specific sign. First, here are a few indispensable crystals to round out your toolkit. These selections are a wonderful support for anyone at any time.

GROUNDING AND PROTECTION

CLEANSING YOUR ENERGY

Smoky Quartz Getting grounded is the basis of spiritual work. So many factors in everyday life pull us out of ourselves. Spending too much time on your phone, not enough time in nature or eating too much sugar are common culprits, but the list goes on. If you want to nail your next meeting at work, remember where your keys are, or get on top of that to-do list, you need to get grounded. Feeling grounded also allows you to be present in your relationships and tuned in to your physical needs. This is where Smoky Quartz can help. This crystal keeps you centred, and emotionally clear. It may help you take a more practical view of a situation. On a more mystical level, Smoky Quartz has the effect of protecting you from energetic drains on your system. It is an excellent protection stone and just holding it can help you feel steady.

Selenite Just as you bathe your body regularly, it makes sense to regularly cleanse your energy system too. Energetic cleansing can help you balance your emotions and clear your mind. Cleanse your energy after work, socializing or spending time in a crowd. Or employ Selenite to help you get rid of emotional residue after a tough conversation. Energy cleansing is also recommended when you are going through any kind of transition – a break-up, a move or some other important milestone. Use Selenite with the intention of purifying your energy field and cleansing yourself of anything that is dragging you down. Imagine that it shines a ray of light through your entire body, clearing and cleansing.

Smoky Quartz Ritual	Selenite Ritual
Perform the grounding practice on page 26 while holding Smoky Quartz to anchor you.	Selenite can also be used to cleanse the energy of your other stones. Place a Selenite stone next to your crystals overnight.

SOOTHING RELAXATION

Rose Quartz We all know what it's like to get stressed out and frazzled. Sometimes the nervous system is overloaded and it's hard to calm down. When that happens, you need a soothing crystal ally that can help you relax. If you are having trouble sleeping, are feeling on edge, or are working through some challenging emotions, it's time to soften with Rose Quartz. This dreamy pink stone is known for its inherent ability to calm and reassure. It soothes you while strengthening your capacity for empathy and compassion. If you're feeling down, lonely or heartbroken, let this crystalline stress-reliever support you.

FINDING YOUR DIRECTION

Clear Quartz Clear quartz is a true all-purpose stone. When you actively set an intention with Clear Quartz, the stone will magnify that intention. When your world is changing around you and you need to forge ahead in a new direction, Clear Quartz will get you there. Clear Quartz can help you clarify, strategize and set your aspirations for your life. Once programmed with your wishes and desires, this powerful amplifier will hold the vibration of your intentions and help you visualize and realize your future.

Rose Quartz Ritual	Clear Quartz Ritual
Infuse a tumbled Rose Quartz stone in your next cup of tea or glass of water for a mindful moment with a soothing elixir.	Write an affirmation that inspires you. Say your affirmation aloud while holding Clear Quartz.

INTUITION
AND INSIGHT

Amethyst   Your intuition is your natural guidance system. It's that gut feeling you have when something feels wrong, or when something feels just right. Intuition shows up in different ways for everyone but it's like a muscle that can be strengthened. If you have questions about your life and you want to tune into the answers, Amethyst is at your service. In those moments, practice asking and listening and let this violet stone help open up your mind's eye. Amethyst is also a fantastic friend when you need help saying the right thing in your next important conversation, meeting or presentation. Or if you are looking for a sparkling boost to your creativity, open the channels of inspiration with Amethyst by your side.

	Amethyst Ritual	

The next time you have a question about your life or
path, lie down and place an Amethyst stone on your forehead or
near the crown of your head. Meditate and make space for
the answer to come through.

THE SIGNS

ASTROLOGY AND YOU

You are a unique being, made up of a solar system of characteristics that define your identity. Astrology illuminates your personality and your path. It describes how you think, learn, love, act and much more. Astrology can also be used to understand the energy of the moment.

Astrology has been contributed to by cultures throughout the world over thousands of years. The astrology used in this book is drawn from contemporary Western astrology. Like all things in the universe, the movements of the planets through the zodiac create a vibration. At the moment of your first breath, this energy is mirrored within you.

Your astrology is much more complex than just your star sign. The movements of the planets under the zodiac, in the exact place, at the exact moment you were born form your birth chart, a personalized map of the sky from your unique vantage point on Earth when you took your first breath. As well as showing you where the Sun lands in your chart, denoting your star sign, it also shows under which signs the Moon and other planets fall – this is the key to understanding your personal energetic code.

In order to discover your unique astrological make-up first you need to map your birth chart.

SUN, MOON AND RISING SIGN

When someone asks, 'What's your sign?' they are actually referring to your Sun sign, but it's worth learning your Moon and Rising signs too. These three symbols are a good place to begin your astrological journey as they represent the basic outline of who you are – like a simple sketch that captures your likeness in just a few brushstrokes. Together these three symbols make up your inner and outer self.

Casting Your Birth Chart Go to www.sandysitron.com/crystals and enter your birth data in the 'Create Your Birth Chart' tool. You'll then receive your birth chart, also called your natal chart, that shows the signs that the planets were in when you were born, and where they were located in the sky.

SUN SIGN

- The Sun is a constant bright light, it symbolizes your ego, the part of you that you consciously identify with. It's how you tend to think of yourself.

- The Sun is the gravitational centre of the solar system, it represents your core self and describes your fundamental character and values.

- The Sun is the energy source that creates life on our planet, it signifies how you channel your energy.

MOON SIGN

The Moon is most visible at night, it symbolizes the part of you that is hard to see – your subconscious self.

The Moon changes shape through the lunar month. It represents your ever-changing emotions and how you respond subconsciously to your feelings.

The Moon is a satellite that circles the Earth, it describes how you turn inwards to protect, nurture and soothe yourself.

RISING SIGN

- The Rising sign, also known as your Ascendant, is the constellation of the zodiac that was rising on the eastern horizon at the precise moment of your birth.

- The Rising sign shines new light into the world. It symbolizes how the rays of your personality beam out ahead as you walk down the street, meet new people, or interact on social media. It represents your vibe or your 'brand'. It epitomizes how other people see you.

- As you explore the following pages, you'll learn how to balance and enhance your unique energy using supportive crystals. This book will also help you find alignment and teach you how to leverage your inherent gifts.

PLANETS

SUN
☉

MOON
☽

MERCURY
☿

VENUS
♀

MARS
♂

JUPITER
♃

SATURN
♄

URANUS
♅

NEPTUNE
♆

PLUTO
♇

DEC 22–JAN 19

JAN 20–FEB 18

FEB 19–MAR 20

MAR 21–APR 19

APR 20–MAY 20

MAY 21–JUN 21

AQUARIUS

CAPRICO

PISCES

ARIES

TAURUS

EMINI

AMETHYST

AQUAMARINE

JASPER

EMERALD

DATES ARE APPROXIMATE AS THE DATES OF THE
SIGNS VARY BY ABOUT A DAY FROM YEAR TO YEAR.

ELEMENTS

FIRE △

EARTH ▽

AIR △

WATER ▽

NOV 22–DEC 21

OCT 24–NOV 21

SEP 23–OCT 23

AUG 23–SEP 22

JUL 23–AUG 22

JUN 22–JUL 22

SAGITTARIUS

SCORPIO

LIBRA

VIRGO

LEO

CANCER

TOPAZ

OPAL

SAPPHIRE

CARNELIAN

MODALITY

CARDINAL ∧

FIXED ⊟

MUTABLE ⌒

TOOLS FOR
YOUR JOURNEY

As you go forwards on your astro-crystal journey,
two key tools can help you gain insight and create positive
change – intuition and intention. Intuition helps you know
what you want and intention helps you make it happen.

LETTING YOUR
INTUITION GUIDE YOU

Everyone is intuitive, your intuition or 'inner knowing' is your built-in guidance system. Use the following prompts to strengthen your inner voice.

How to Connect with Your Intuition

Slow down   Take a few deep breaths and close your eyes. The more you can slow down in your life (even for just five minutes) the louder your intuitive voice grows.

Pose a question   What do you want to know? Ask yourself. Say it aloud or ponder it silently. Or choose to write it down, sketch it or even dance it out. However you pose the question, make sure it is clear. If you aren't sure what to ask, try, 'what do I need to know that I don't yet know?'

Listen for the answer   You might hear words or notice a sensation in your body. You might write down your question in a notebook then flip the page and write down the answer. You might have an emotional response or feel compelled to move in a certain way. Pay attention.

Practice   The more you practice asking and listening, the more you get to understand your unique intuitive voice. Just as weightlifting tones your physical body, practicing these steps improves your intuitive muscle, so stick with it!

INTENTION
SETTING

In your meditations and rituals, you can program your crystals with the intentions or affirmations that will help you meet your goals.

An intention is a new thought that you would like to think. Our subconscious minds save energy by putting certain thoughts and habits on repeat. This survival skill has benefits, such as giving us more energy and space for other things, but it also has its downsides, such as getting us stuck in a negative pattern. One way to break in a new way of thinking is to intentionally repeat a new thought. Here is how to 'affirm' your new way of thinking into being!

Define what it is you would like to change. Where are you feeling stuck? What is the pattern that is bugging you? For example, 'I am stuck because I have these exciting ideas for new projects, but I never finish what I start.'

- <u>Decide what you want</u>
  For instance, 'It would be great if I finished my projects.'

- <u>Make it an 'I' statement</u>
  Such as, 'I finish my projects.'

- <u>Make it affirmative</u>
  Make sure your affirmation is positively stated. Say what you want, not what you don't want. So 'I finish my projects' not 'I no longer leave my projects unfinished'.

- <u>Make it in the here and now</u>
  Write your affirmation in the present tense: 'I finish my projects' rather than 'I will finish my projects'.

- <u>Describe the feeling</u>
  Include some positive descriptors, so that you can easily visualize how great it feels to realize your affirmation: 'I finish my projects and I feel so satisfied.'

- <u>Evaluate</u> Does the affirmation you wrote give you a positive feeling? If so, wonderful! You have your affirmation. If not, refine it. You may need a 'stepping stone' to make your affirmation more believable. For example, if you have a complicated track record with finishing what you begin, your subconscious mind may need more help believing 'I finish my projects and I feel so satisfied'. In that case try, 'I believe in the possibility that I finish my projects and feel satisfied', or 'I'm learning to finish my projects with satisfaction and ease'. With time and practice you'll find that you no longer need the stepping stone and you can update your affirmation to 'I easily finish my projects and I'm filled with satisfaction!'

WAYS TO
WORK WITH
CRYSTALS

Crystals are a powerful force as they are but,
in order to optimize their benefits, discover how
to care for and recharge them with regular
cleansing, and learn how to activate them using
the intentions you've developed.

CLEANSE YOUR CRYSTALS

Everything on Earth must go through a
process of decay and renewal. Cleansing your
crystals can help them reset with a clear energetic
frequency. When you cleanse a crystal, imagine
that you are clearing it of any energy that it may
have picked up from yourself, other people
and the environment.

How to Cleanse Your Crystals

Make sure to research your stone to discover if the method you are considering is safe for both you and the crystal. For example, some crystals may dissolve in water or fade in sunlight. Some stones contain trace minerals that may be physically harmful when released into water.

Light: Place your crystal in sunlight or moonlight for an hour.
Salt: Immerse your crystal in salt for about five minutes.
Sound: Chant or use an instrument such as singing bowls, chimes or tuning forks.
Water: Wash your crystal under running water, from a natural water source or a tap, for a few minutes.
Visualization: Imagine crystalline light or archangels surrounding your crystal with the intention of cleansing.
Selenite: Place selenite next to your crystal and leave in place overnight.
Earth: Bury your crystal underground for about a day.

When to cleanse your crystals

It's a good idea to cleanse your crystal when you first get it and about once a month after that. Cleanse more often if you use your crystals regularly.

GROUND
YOURSELF

Before you do any kind of energy work, it's important to get grounded. When a ship puts down its anchor in a quiet harbour, it's protected from being pulled by strong waves back into the sea. As you engage in energy work with crystals, you may drift and dream far afield. It protects you to have an anchor that keeps you connected to the Earth.

How to Get
Grounded

- To begin, set yourself up in a quiet and comfortable space, either seated or lying down. Close your eyes. Imagine that your torso is like a tree trunk with roots growing down through your feet.

- Breathe comfortably and deeply as you imagine your roots flowing down through the ground and all the way to the Earth's core.

- Visualize a healing light moving up through your roots into your body. Imagine this healing light circulating through your body and carrying any tension or stress away and out, and back down into the Earth.

- Continue to imagine the energy flow – grounding energy coming up through your roots, tension and stress flowing back down to the Earth.

- When you feel relaxed and grounded, give thanks to the Earth before you open your eyes.

ACTIVATE YOUR CRYSTALS

Now that your crystal is cleansed and you are grounded, you can 'program' your crystal with the intention you've developed. Programming your crystal is one way to activate it so that its vibrations are attuned to your desires and goals. It's as simple as telling your crystal what you intend to create or achieve.

How to Program Your Intention

To amplify your crystal's power, focus your thoughts on your intention and rain that energy towards your crystal.

Make sure you have a clear intention or affirmation.

Set a timer for ten minutes.

Sit comfortably either in a chair or on the floor.

Hold your crystal or place it on your body. You could also place it on the floor or on a table in front of you.

- On each inhale, repeat your intention out loud or in your mind.

- On each exhale bring your attention to your crystal.

- When you notice your attention wandering, bring your awareness back to the crystal and your breath.

- Repeat until your timer sounds.

SAGITTARIUS

DATES: NOVEMBER 22–DECEMBER 21 ELEMENT: FIRE
MODALITY: MUTABLE PLANET: JUPITER SYMBOL: ARCHER
CRYSTAL: RUBY

YOUR SIGN, EXPLAINED

Bold, thoughtful, unsinkable Sagittarius. Your sign's symbol is a Centaur who is an archer. The Centaur is half human, half horse, and so Sagittarius represents both wisdom and wildness. You aim for the highest understanding and education. And you love nature, freedom, wilderness and sports.

The Archer shoots the arrow up into the sky, aiming for the highest ideals and most potent philosophies. As a Sagittarius, you seek to broaden your understanding of life and the world – through travel, education and spirituality. Your zest for life is infinite and you use your passion to explore all facets of existence. You have a naturally optimistic spirit that helps you float through life.

Based on your learnings and explorations, you form bold opinions, and you aren't too shy to share them! You are sure in your beliefs and you let that knowledge guide you. Because your sign is mutable and adaptable, you also know that it's OK to update your opinions, as you are always learning.

There are no limits to the possibilities that await buoyant Sagittarius. You have a glass-half-full attitude, so you scan situations for potential and opportunity. A natural cheerleader, you know how to pump up the crowd and get a group excited. When you truly believe in something, your infectious energy makes it easy for you to sell that idea or product to others.

Enlightened, adventurous and cheerful, you know how to enjoy the journey, and you aren't afraid to take a risk when necessary.

SAGITTARIUS IS A
FIRE SIGN

Fire ignites the spirit – it's the spark of life, the twinkle in your eyes. Creative and dynamic, you have a strong connection with your fiery life force. You shine with vibrancy and vivacity and are focused on living life to the fullest.

SAGITTARIUS IS A
TRANSPERSONAL SIGN

Transpersonal signs extend beyond the personal to live and work for the benefit of all people. These signs tend to consider the big picture and can factor other people's feelings and experiences into their own beliefs, goals and dreams.

SAGITTARIUS IS A
MUTABLE SIGN

The Mutable signs adapt and refine. This energy helps you constantly learn. You define and redefine your ever-changing beliefs and philosophies.

SAGITTARIUS IS RULED BY
THE PLANET JUPITER

The largest of the planets, Jupiter is expansive and bestows a generous, lucky and optimistic energy to Sagittarius.

THE CENTAUR IS THE
SYMBOL FOR SAGITTARIUS

The half-wise and half-wild Centaur, who is an archer, takes aim at high ideals.

RUBY IS A KEY
CRYSTAL BIRTHSTONE
FOR SAGITTARIUS

Ruby is a potent crystal for all Sagittarius people. Both cheery and courageous, fire-red Ruby gets you motivated. Choose it as your go-to support when you need a boost of extra strength, or when you need some encouragement. Ruby is the best of cheerleaders, helping you feel good about yourself so that you can reach for your goals.

SAGITTARIUS
TRAITS

Your key traits show how you shine.
These are the special characteristics
that make you unique.

Go-getting   Fiery and visionary, you can
imagine great goals, and muster up the
courage to go for them! These qualities
make you an ambitious achiever.

Wild   You're freedom-seeking and
spirited. You aren't held back by rules,
and you prefer to choose your own
path. A nature-lover at heart, you enjoy
exploring the wilderness.

Positive   A natural optimist, you tend
to see situations in a positive light.

Receptive   Before you form your
famous opinions, you are open-minded
and receptive. You enjoy exploring all
possibilities. You are adaptable, so when
new information enters your field you
take it in and assess it for yourself.

Enthusiastic   When you believe
in something, you are full of ardent
appreciation and enthusiastic energy.

Wise   Your penchant for asking the big
questions and your nonstop desire to
learn and grow give you great wisdom.

Honest   Although you love to
exaggerate when you're telling a fun story
you are deeply honest and principled.
You are fuelled by your search for a
greater truth about the universe.

Adaptable   You love to learn and
are capable of applying your mind to
many different kinds of endeavours. In
addition, you love to change and keep
moving forwards. All of these qualities
make you adaptable and versatile.

SAGITTARIUS GIFTS
AND GROWTH AREAS

Your natural gifts offer both strengths and
challenges. The same traits that make you
special may also require balance at times.

ascinated vs Fanatical   When you
g into a topic that fascinates you, you
ecome truly enthusiastic. At moments,
our enthusiasm for your ideas can
erge on being too zealous or fanatical.

elieving vs Blind   You are so positive
nd optimistic. Sometimes that tendency
an blind you to potential pitfalls.

ucky vs Lazy   It's not that you're
pathetic or lethargic. It's just that you
re so lucky, and you pull things off
ith such little effort, that you might
times get a bit lazy. Why work hard
hen rewards come so easily?

Wanderlust vs Wandering   You love
to travel and explore. When you can't
actually do that, you may find that
your mind wanders or that you feel
a bit restless. If you're not actively
moving ahead, you can quickly feel as
if you're languishing.

Truthful vs Tactless   Fiercely
opinionated, you aren't afraid to be
honest about what you think. While
this straightforward attitude can be
refreshing, at times it might come off as
a bit blunt or tactless.

Carefree vs Careless   You have a
breezy, carefree attitude. But if your
blithe, lighthearted nature causes you
to skip over important details, you
might find that you've been hasty or
reckless. Be mindful of impulsiveness
or lack of self-discipline leading to
irresponsible tendencies.

Compatibility is a complex feature of astrology because you are more than just your Sun sign. And other people are multi-faceted too.

Friends

Aries provides the spark that ignites your spirit. Life together is like a never-ending fireworks display.

You and **Leo** are like racehorses rounding the track. By giving it your all, you inspire each other to push forwards.

Libra lets you talk and philosophize to your heart's content. If you're lucky, they might even be up for a lively debate!

There are no limits to the dreams you can envision with inventive **Aquarius** by your side.

Foes

Taurus stays the course, while you'd rather explore uncharted territory. Sagittarius needs to move forwards and change things up, while **Taurus** enjoys routines.

Your wild side stresses **Cancer** out, and it's hard for you to find the patience needed to help the Crab through a tough day.

Scorpio wants to let their emotion marinate, while you'd rather fire up the grill and move on.

Capricorn's heavy sense of responsibility can weigh down your high spirits. The Goat is inspired by duty and work, while Sagittarius prefers to feel free and unhindered.

♈	♎	♉	♏
ARIES	LIBRA	TAURUS	SCORPIO
♌	♒	♋	♑
LEO	AQUARIUS	CANCER	CAPRICORN

SAGITTARIUS SUN

If you were born November 22–December 21, Sagittarius is your Sun sign (check your birth chart for an exact calculation). Your Sun sign describes your basic energy.

Just as the Sun is the centre of the solar system, your Sun sign (also called your zodiac sign or star sign) symbolizes the core of your being. As a Sagittarius Sun, you deeply value independence, honesty and curiosity. Travel and higher education allow you to open your mind and explore the truth of the human experience. You yearn to grow and expand by asking the big questions about life.

At times, you need to remember that, as much as you like to explore the outer world, the answers you seek are already within you. When you can slow down and explore your emotions, you discover important truths about yourself.

Because your Sun sign fuels your confidence and enlivens your sense of self, there are two recommended crystals for Sagittarius Sun. The Amplifying crystal will help you expand upon your gifts and the Balancing crystal will help you integrate your growth areas.

SAGITTARIUS SUN AMPLIFYING CRYSTAL

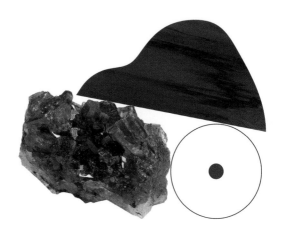

ENTHUSIASM, ADVENTURE, COURAGE

Ruby Sagittarius, your great gifts are your love of adventure and your stirring enthusiasm. Ruby is your perfect match. This intense red corundum mineral highlights your best qualities and amplifies them back to you. It will help you follow your heart to the people, projects and adventures that will light you up and make you feel fulfilled.

If you ever need a little extra sparkle, carry this flame-red crystal by your side. It may help boost your courage so that you feel lit up and ready for anything. You are at your best when you can be spontaneous and have fun, and this courageous stone can help you trust yourself to take the chances that come your way.

You tend to be optimistic, but if you ever have doubts that you can't shake, call on Ruby to boost your spirits and help you see the bright side again. This powerful crystal can give you an encouraging push forwards when you need it most.

SAGITTARIUS SUN BALANCING CRYSTAL

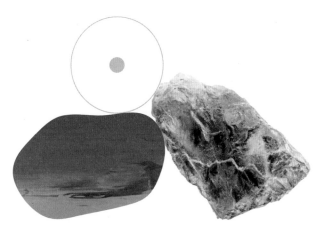

**INNER TRUTH, PEACE,
PURPOSE**

Iolite Your life's purpose is very important to you. As your sign loves to explore the outer world, through travel, adventure and education, it may seem natural to seek outside of yourself for clues to your purpose. However, this can leave you feeling derailed. Iolite helps balance this impulse by letting you remember that you already have the answers you seek, and that to find them you must slow down and look within.

This dreamy and calming cordierite mineral may help you connect to your higher self through meditation and self-reflection. It amplifies your naturally keen intuition and helps you understand the language of your inner world.

Iolite boosts your sense of peace and joy so that your natural enthusiasm is heightened. This cobalt-blue stone warms your heart by helping you connect with your inner truth.

SAGITTARIUS MOON

CLARITY, COMMUNICATION, CONFIDENCE

In the same way that the Moon always appears to be changing shape in the sky, the Moon in your chart symbolizes the part of you that is always changing – your emotions.

Imagine that when you have an emotion come up, the Sagittarius part of you steps to centre stage. This happens throughout the day. It doesn't matter if the emotion is happiness, sadness, frustration or exhilaration – when emotions arise you go into full Sagittarius mode. Your spontaneous, adventurous, philosophical, honest, bold and enthusiastic side is accentuated. You are fiercely freedom-loving and you are motivated to ask big questions about life and existence.

As a Sagittarius Moon, you react with gusto. When spurred by emotion, you tend to have big, larger-than-life reactions. You are so passionate about what you believe that at times you may even be a bit blunt.

Your love of adventure and freedom sparks up when you're emotional, driving you to leave the past behind

you and carry on to the next adventure. Because you love to move forwards, at times you need to remember to slow down and process your feelings.

Your bouncy optimism is uplifting and inspiring, but when your emotions are high, you may go overboard with your opinions. You are most supported by a crystal that helps you communicate your feelings with wisdom and clarity.

Blue Topaz This cool blue silicate mineral helps you do what you love best – follow your own path. This crystal is like a light in the dark, so let it open up your mind to greater understanding about who you are and where you're going. Blue Topaz may help you focus, connect and enjoy mental clarity.

A gentle and soothing stone, Blue Topaz can help you communicate your truth with gracious harmony. With this crystalline bolster to your confidence, any fears you may have around communication can dissolve. Share you thoughts and beliefs with others through genuine communication.

SAGITTARIUS RISING

WISDOM, SERENITY, PROTECTION

Your Rising Sign is the sign that was on the eastern horizon when you were born. It represents the face you show to the world – your social personality. As a Sagittarius Rising, you pulse with enthusiasm and joy. When you enter a room, your vibe is upbeat and generous. You know that life is too short to hold back, and you might as well look on the bright side. With this vivacious energy, you inspire others to join in the fun and follow you on amusing adventures.

Other people perceive you to be simultaneously bold and thoughtful. You're strong-willed and boisterous, but also philosophical and profound.

When it comes to group endeavours, you show strong leadership potential. Because you're keen on defining your values, other people are inspired by your unique philosophies. On the rare occasion that no-one wants to follow your direction, you're confident striking out on your own.

As a Sagittarius Rising, you benefit from a crystal that affirms your connection with your truth, your wisdom and your life purpose.

Turquoise You yearn to share your truth with the world. When you have a great idea or a profound insight, it feels good to teach and share these wisdoms. Turquoise is a stone of wisdom and communication, making it your perfect ally in your quest to know your heart and connect with others.

This blue–green or sky-blue stone in the phosphate group of minerals has long been used for its protective and calming qualities. By offering a buffer to the outer world, this supportive and soothing crystal helps you tune into your inner world and define who you are. You love nothing more than to bound forwards and take on new challenges, and with Turquoise by your side, you'll know when these adventures are aligned with your heart.

OTHER SAGITTARIUS SUPPORT CRYSTALS

The following crystals are helpful for all Sagittarius placements – your Sun, Moon, Rising Sign and any other Sagittarius planet or point you may have in your chart. Harness the potential of these stones for clarity and ease in important life areas.

Everyone has different goals for romantic love. In addition, your wishes or desires can change over time. You may wish to attract or pursue love. Perhaps you are hoping to deepen your ability to love, or to open up to intimacy physically, emotionally or spiritually. As a Sagittarius, you believe that a loving relationship should be growth-oriented with both people ever evolving and learning. You love to have a good time in your relationships. This is an area where your natural optimism, spontaneity and sense of adventure really shine. Every moment spent with you feels like a dynamic and vitalizing experience.

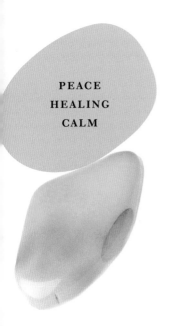

**PEACE
HEALING
CALM**

Pink Opal   Pink Opal is a beneficial stone for Sagittarius as it helps you embrace your open, fun and loving side. It lightens the mood and dissolves any fears you may have. Like all Opals, it promotes emotional healing, protection and peacefulness. You thrive when your relationships are expansive and progressing. That's a wonderful thing, but sometimes your forward-moving energy can foster a restless state of searching. Soft, rose-coloured Pink Opal can gently remind you that it's also nice to enjoy the moment, relax and be present. You have everything you need.

43

SAGITTARIUS × FRIENDSHIP

Friends offer support, fun, love and new perspectives. With Sagittarius prominently placed in your chart, you bring a wave of upbeat optimism to your friendships. Your charisma, enthusiasm and bravery remind others that life is meant to be lived fully! Your light is like a beacon of fun and adventure, and others are drawn to your warmth. You love to do fun activities with your friends, but time spent probing the deeper questions and philosophies of life is also very important to you. If you've been known to show up late one too many times, or flake on commitments, your friendships may be supported by a crystal that helps you act more responsibly.

Smoky Quartz You dive headfirst into your friendships, so when you need to tone it down and be a bit more discerning, Smoky Quartz can help you figure out who to listen to or team up with. This tawny Quartz is an excellent grounding stone, which helps you root your sometimes flaky attitude, relieve stress and communicate calmly. If you tend to fly off the handle and say the wrong thing, this stone may help you collect yourself and speak with compassion. Your friendships will benefit from the dose of responsibility that Smoky Quartz can provide. Additionally, it amplifies your naturally positive nature.

**GROUNDED
RELIABLE
DISCERNING**

strological insight can galvanize your money-making potential. Your Sagittarius prosperity fts are generosity, leadership, risk-taking nd enthusiasm. If you'd like to make more noney, look to these qualities for inspiration. Vhat aligns with your values? How can ou take the lead? Sagittarius tends to be enerally relaxed about money and often has subconscious belief that money comes and oes. If this is you, you may benefit from a exible budgeting system. Your ability to take sks is one of your greatest financial strengths s it allows you an entrepreneurial spirit. You re always willing to put yourself out there, nd generally your efforts are rewarded with ick and success. When you fail, you quickly ounce back and move on.

SAGITTARIUS ×
MONEY

**POSITIVITY
RESPONSIBILITY
WISDOM**

Yellow Sapphire   This butter-yellow gemstone is a first-rate prosperity stone. Sagittarians are known to be lucky, and this charm of a crystal may increase your good fortune. It's a subtly grounding stone that also has a positive and uplifting energy. This is a profitable combination, helping you to both hone your self-discipline and stay open to new possibilities. With Yellow Sapphire by your side, you may feel more clear-sighted and wise as you make solid decisions for your financial future.

Sagittarius, you've got energy and drive. Your fires are ignited when you feel passionately about the work you're doing. Imaginative and creative, you're a lifelong learner. Think of yourself as an explorer or philosopher – you like to do work that feels expansive and is thought-provoking. You may even choose to work in travel or education, although many vocations call to you. As long as your work provides freedom, fun and plenty of opportunities, you're all in. You thrive on deadlines and other pressurized, high-stakes situations. Anything that gets your adrenaline going will spark your fiery engines. However you need to create work–life balance because travel and exploration help you keep your positive perspective of life.

Sodalite   Let Sodalite enhance your keen intellect and sense of purpose. This midnight-blue tectosilicate mineral helps you know yourself. It amplifies your intuition so that you feel aligned with your path and purpose. Your career and work life thrive when you know what you want and have the energy to go after it. Sodalite encourages 'aha' moments that blast open your perspective so that you can see the big picture. With this rich blue stone by your side you can fully trust yourself to make excellent decisions at work. And as an added benefit, it reduces stress and promotes serenity, which is good news when you need to turn down the hustle and relax.

**INTUITION
INNER-KNOWING
PURPOSE**

Your mutable fire sign is elastic and high-spirited. You've got a bouncy attitude, which means that nothing can keep you down – including physical or mental ailments. For the most part you are robust and generally healthy. Lucky Jupiter is your sign's ruler, and that's a blessing for your health and well-being. Sports and athletics are fun for you – you enjoy using your body and you take good care of it. You also love to live large! That might mean running a marathon, or conversely, it could mean overindulging in your favourite treat. Learning to be more moderate is something you may decide to aim for. Slowing down can help you be more deliberate, calm any excess nervous energy and even break a cycle of overworking.

HEALTHY HABITS
FOCUS
GROUNDING

Vesuvianite   Vesuvianite (also called Idocrase) is a silicate mineral found in a range of colours: purple, green, brown, and even red. This stunning stone helps you settle down and focus, especially when it comes to following through on the healthy changes and good habits that you determine to be in your best interest. With Vesuvianite by your side you can release outdated patterns that may be affecting your health and well-being. Reach for this crystal when you want to feel grounded or when you want support in strengthening your mind–body connection.

SAGITTARIUS
THROUGHOUT
THE YEAR

he energies of the zodiac signs affect us throughout the ear. In astrology, there is a season for everything. Feeling eparated from nature's cycles and rhythms can make you eel out of step or off-kilter. It may add to stress and drain nergy. Understanding and attuning to astrology's seasons ight help you feel enlivened.

Take this attunement one step further by using crystals to mplify the unique energy of each moment, so that you feel lly aligned with the rhythms of nature.

The following pages take you on a journey with the sun s it passes through the twelve signs of the zodiac on its nnual rotation. You will discover the key energies of each eason, along with a sign-specific horoscope that aligns with e important themes of your unique chart.

CONFIDENCE AND LEADERSHIP

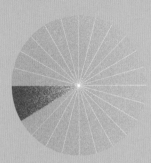

Aries season is the signal that begins the horse race. And they're off! This is the moment to gallop at top speed towards your goals. Put yourself out there with confidence. Make bold decisions and step in time with your intuition. This season is about saying YES to who you are and living your life with freedom. The buds are beginning to emerge and new life is beginning. Sync up with this feeling of potential and possibility.

SAGITTARIUS HOROSCOPE FOR ARIES SEASON

Connect with your true self during Aries season. The Sun is lighting up your zone of creativity, self-expression and love. There's no better time to put yourself centre stage. Shine brightly, whatever way makes you happy! Enjo life with the wonder and curiosity of a child.

Morning Practice

Get your heart rate up with
some fiery cardio exercise.

Evening Practice

Cool down that inner
fire with a soothing herbal tea.

CRYSTALS FOR
ARIES SEASON

CONFIDENCE

Hessonite Garnet   Developing confidence is a practice of
establishing deep self-trust. Let Hessonite Garnet's activating
and powerful energy help you build up your courage so that
you can just go for it. Also try Green Aventurine, Orange
Calcite or Malachite.

LIVING BOLDLY

Pink Aventurine   When the time is ripe for taking bold
action, Pink Aventurine can help you advance into your next
adventure. Reach for it when you need a boost of fun. This
spirited crystal connects you with your heart centre, and acts
as your best accomplice in bravery and boldness. Or choose
Ruby, Tangerine Quartz or Sardonyx.

DRIVE

Fire Agate   Aries season is the vehicle in which to follow
your passions and desires, which makes Fire Agate the
gasoline. Whether you need to get an important project
going or just tackle spring cleaning, put yourself on track to
get things done by syncing up with the vibration of this fierce
crystal. You could also reach for Bloodstone, Stromatolite
or Cinabrite.

MONEY AND
SELF-WORTH

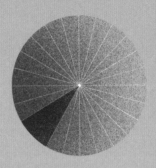

Like working in a garden and then enjoying the beauty that you've cultivated, Taurus represents sustained effort that leads to a productive reward. This season is the prime time to focus on building up your sense of personal worth and value. On one level, this process may involve nurturing you self-esteem. On another level, this may include thinking about security, money and finances. Taurus season is also a time to remember the beauty of life. It reminds us that no matter what is going on, there are simple pleasures to be had

SAGITTARIUS HOROSCOPE
FOR TAURUS SEASON

Find a routine that works for you. The Sun is moving through your sector of habits, workflows, health and service. Get organized and apply a flexible yet productive structure to your day.

If there are health issues that you've been ignoring, this is a great time to give your body some attention and ta proactive measures so that you can fe your best.

Morning Practice	**Evening Practice**
Practice gratitude by reminding yourself of three things you're grateful for.	Do something that feels good to your body, like stretching or wearing soft clothing.

CRYSTALS FOR TAURUS SEASON

MONEY MAGIC

Green Jade No matter where you are beginning financially, Green Jade will juice up your money situation. This abundance stone has a way of amplifying your potential. A soft and expansive prosperity stone that soothes the spirit, it will support you as you make wise financial decisions. Reach for it when you crave a feeling of security. You could also use Pyrite, Emerald or Epidote.

SELF-WORTH

Red Jasper Red Jasper will amp up your self-appreciation quotient. Choose Red Jasper when you're feeling uncertain, if your confidence could use a boost, or if you want to feel more resilient in any way. This stone will get you in the groove of trusting your own value. Also try Carnelian, Chrysocolla or Bixbite.

ABUNDANCE

Green Apatite If you are feeling like something in your life is lacking, such as money, time, energy, sleep, or support, for example, you might need to boost your sense of abundance. Taurus season is the perfect time to grasp hold of that feeling of nature's plentifulness. Use Green Apatite to replenish your energy and help you feel satisfied and satiated with what you have. You could also reach for Golden Tourmaline, Uvarovite Garnet or Agate.

VALUES
AND COMMUNITY

Gemini energy is like a buzzing bee that moves from flower to flower in a garden. This season is a time of mental stimulation, new ideas, learning, communicating and sharing. Use Gemini season to evaluate or challenge your mindset and values. Which attitudes are no longer serving you? What's truly important to you? Gemini season is also a time to connect with others in the community. What can you learn from others? What can you teach others? It's a fun and lively season full of new connections.

SAGITTARIUS HOROSCOPE
FOR GEMINI SEASON

The Sun is moving through your area of partnership. Think about your most important relationships. Are they balanced, or is something feeling lopsided? Think about giving and receiving. There may be compromises to make or conversations to have. What has been left unsaid? This is a good time to take care of yourself and contemplate your goals and desires in your relationships.

Morning Practice

Help a new mindset
emerge with a potent Gemini
season intention.

Evening Practice

Before falling asleep, envision
yourself having a great time at a party
surrounded by everyone you love.

CRYSTALS FOR
GEMINI SEASON

MASTER YOUR MINDSET

Heliodor   Have repeating thoughts, fears or anxieties been
plaguing you? Use the revitalizing energy of Gemini season and
Heliodor to hit the reset button on these old thought patterns.
This stone will gently help you harmonize your thoughts and
adjust your mindset, helping you reconnect with your true
values. Alternatively, try Blue Lace Agate, Chrome Chalcedony
or Dragonstone.

CONNECTING

Agatized Coral   When you really want to feel connected,
seen, heard and understood, reach for Agatized Coral. This
fossilized coral nudges you to reach out to others and helps you
analyse your relationships, whether with friends, lovers, family,
neighbours or colleagues. It relays an upbeat feeling so that you
can view your relationships with the people in your life with
optimism. You may also choose Citrine, Apricot Agate
or Bismuth.

COMMUNICATION

Aquamarine   Aquamarine is your crystal-clear
communication companion. Communication helps us feel
connected, and allows us to learn and grow. In those moments
when you feel confused or foggy, this elegant stone will help
you become grounded and steady. Use Aquamarine to find
your voice – it will help you tune into your own true message
and the truth of those around you. Alternatively, reach for
Turquoise, Prairie Tanzanite or Green Chrysocolla.

HOME AND NURTURE

Come on home to Cancer season. Like Cancer's symbol, the Crab, wrap yourself in a protective shell and reflect on your life and your feelings. In Cancer season, engage in meaningful self-care, and also put your energy into nurturing others. Discover what makes you feel safe and cosy. This could be your actual home, your closest relationships or tending to the feelings and needs of your inner child.

SAGITTARIUS HOROSCOPE FOR CANCER SEASON

This is an emotional season. The Sun is travelling through your area of intimacy, transformation and forgiveness. Think about the cycles that are ending and beginning now. Maybe there is an opportunity to process and release emotions that have been weighing on your heart. Make space for yourself and allow yourself to feel your feelings during this tender time.

Morning Practice	Evening Practice
Let your inner child take the lead: what do they want to do today?	Sing a lullaby to soothe your inner child before bed.

CRYSTALS FOR CANCER SEASON

NURTURING

Blue Calcite   What do you want to actively care for?
Yourself? A child? A creative project? In order to feel truly
nurturing, you need to feel inspired by love. Blue Calcite will
help you soften and open up your heart centre, so that you
feel drawn to put your compassionate and attentive energy
where it is needed most. Other nurturing crystals include
Moonstone, Blue Chalcedony and Bumblebee Jasper.

HOME ENVIRONMENT

Pink Mangano Calcite   Home is where you are safe and
protected. It's your emotional nest where you can relax. Use
Pink Mangano Calcite to create a grounded and peaceful
home environment. This stone acts as a balm that will help
you feel harmonized. Place this rosy crystal in your inner
sanctum and set the intention to soothe conflict and soften
your environment so that you can restore your energy after a
long day or week. You could also try Chiastolite, Rose Quartz
or Peach Moonstone.

FAMILY BONDS

Bornite   Family, whether chosen or blood-related, represent
some of our closest relationships. Use Bornite to foster the
strength of family relationships. This is a joyful stone that
will help you embrace the positives that come from your
family circle, while at the same time grounding you to help
you remember who you are as an individual. Also try Orange
Calcite, Indigo Gabbro or Girasol Quartz.

CREATIVITY AND FUN

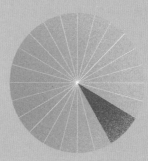

Harnessing your creativity and expressing your true self with others, that's the key to making the most of Leo season. It's all about playful sharing and creative shining. Radiate your magnificent heart of gold outwards with immediacy, freedom, spontaneity, generosity and a giant sense of fun. During this season of wholehearted self-expression, take a little time to remember how unique you are. Remember what inspires you and reflect on what you love most about yourself.

SAGITTARIUS HOROSCOPE FOR LEO SEASON

Take advantage of this excellent time to explore and learn. Open your mind to new possibilities. The Sun is moving through your area of travel, philosophy and higher learning. What lights you up? Maybe inspiration comes from visiting a new place or reading a book of poetry. Use this season to remember that anything is possible.

Affirmation

MY CREATIVE SELF IS
COMING OUT TO PLAY.

Morning Practice

Create daily.

Evening Practice

Seek out a chance to laugh every day and go to bed with a smile on your face.

INSPIRATION

Rutilated Quartz   Inspiration is the creative spark and Rutilated Quartz can help you turn that spark into a roaring bonfire. Make Leo season feel lit up with creativity. Keep Rutilated Quartz by your side when you need an inventive solution to a problem at work, when your love life could use an inspiring reboot, or when you are ready to awaken the artist within. Set your intentions and let this highly programmable stone carry the flame of your dreams. You could also use Sunstone, Golden Labradorite or Yellow Sapphire.

SELF-APPRECIATION

Thulite   Leo season is the time to shed all insecurities and put your faith in your one true self. Loving yourself dissolves insecurity and self-criticism. Thulite tunes you into the vibration of love, peace and harmony, allowing you to be present and wholly yourself. Alternatively, reach for Ruby, Larimar, or Desert Jasper.

COURAGE

Golden Apatite   To ensure your lion-heartedness knows no bounds, you need to fire up your courage. Golden Apatite bestows upon you both passion and discernment, which determine which fears are baseless. Use it when you need to take a risk at work, strike up a conversation with someone you admire or stand up for your values. Other courage-giving crystals are Carnelian, Iolite-Sunstone or Citrine.

HEALTH
AND HABITS

Our goals and dreams require a big-picture view,
but Virgo season reminds us that life is actually lived in the
small details. Focus on how you are living your life, your
everyday routines and rituals. On a practical level, what is
important to you? Virgo energy helps you take a closer
look at your health and habits, and how you can be
of service to others as well.

SAGITTARIUS HOROSCOPE
FOR VIRGO SEASON

With the Sun moving through your zone of career, this is a great moment to be productive. You may find that it's easier right now to make plans and create strategies at work. Use this high-energy time to the fullest by putting yourself out there and making things happen in your career or vocation.

Affirmation
I CREATE HEALTHY HABITS.

Morning Practice	**Evening Practice**
Drink a glass of water first thing.	Write down one task you're going to complete tomorrow, and stick to it.

FOCUS

Clear Quartz   Virgo season ushers in a chance to notice the details and get focused. Use Clear Quartz to take you all the way there. This cleansing stone helps you rivet your attention on your commitments. When you program Clear Quartz with your intention for focus, you'll find that it supports you, whether you have a tight deadline or you just really need to concentrate. You could also turn to Vanadinite, Amazonite or Tiger Iron.

HEALTH

Chevron Amethyst   A lot of factors go into maintaining optimum health: genetics, diet, exercise, access to care, to name just a few. Virgo season energy will encourage you to think wisely about the preventative measures that you can take to boost both your mental well-being and physical health. Use Chevron Amethyst for gentle motivation that can help you happily embrace healthier choices. Or try Girasol Quartz, Ruby Fuchsite or Black Tourmaline.

ALTRUISM

Stromatolite   Humanity wouldn't be a successful species without the desire to be of service to others. Virgo season plus Stromatolite is your recommendation for kindness and selfless action. Turn your attention to what you can do to help others, whether that's volunteering, making a donation to a good cause, or simply smiling and being friendly. Let Stromatolite amplify your altruistic nature. Alternatively, reach for Stichtite, Rhodonite or Rose Quartz.

RELATIONSHIPS AND BALANCE

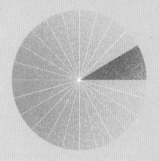

Libra season is symbolized by balanced scales.
It's a chance to look at all life areas and judge the
equilibrium. Are your relationships in balance? Do both
people in your relationships have what they want and
need? This can be a fun and harmonious time to socialize.
During Libra season, balance can also be created in your
environment through art, decoration and organization.
The scales are the symbol for justice and Libra season bring
a collective yearning to make the systems of government
more fair and to expose inequalities.

SAGITTARIUS HOROSCOPE FOR LIBRA SEASON

Dream big, Sagittarius. The Sun is
traversing your sector of hopes and
visions for the future. Be inventive and
creative. What future do you see for
yourself? Who do you want in your
community? How do you want to
change the world? Use your imaginatio
and explore the possibilities.

Morning Practice

Reach out and message
someone who is important to
you, and tell them why.

Evening Practice

Meditate to create
mental balance.

CRYSTALS FOR
LIBRA SEASON

HEALTHY BOUNDARIES

Iolite   Communicating what you want, need and desire is a
great starting point to gain clarity in your relationships. Iolite
can help you reflect and get to know yourself – the first step to
speaking and sharing your truth with others. Once your inner
base is stabilized, Iolite can help you reach out to another
person, while maintaining your own healthy boundaries. This
healing stone has a peaceful energy that helps you create
balance between yourself and a partner. You could also use
Amazonite, Purple Jade or Chiastolite.

BALANCE

Shungite   Balance is an active state, requiring constant
adjustment. It comes under the jurisdiction of the intellectual,
analytical sign of Libra. Keep checking in with yourself
throughout Libra season to determine what needs more
balance. For a crystal that will help you stay steady, reach for
Shungite. Or choose Diopside, Selenite or Turquoise.

DECISIVENESS

Ametrine   Libra season is an excellent time to analyse, think
things through and come up with new ideas. Keep Ametrine
by your desk for productive planning sessions and for when you
have big decisions to make. This balancing stone will help you
keep your life on track. As an alternative, try Variscite, Fluorite
or White Sapphire.

TRANSFORMATION AND FORGIVENESS

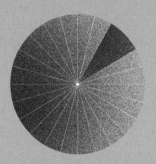

Scorpio season pulls you deeper – emotionally, physically and spiritually. This is a season of transformation, helping you to feel deeply, release old emotions and thought patterns, and get ready to move on to the next stage. By pulling back the layers and being honest with the truth of who you are, it's also an opportunity to deepen your relationships with others by letting them get to know the real you.

SAGITTARIUS HOROSCOPE FOR SCORPIO SEASON

The Sun is moving through your area of reflection and intuition during Scorpio season. Retreat and connect with your true self during this dreamy season. Explore your spiritual life. This would be a great opportunity to try meditation. Find quiet time, away from distractions and technology, even if it's just for a few minutes a day.

Morning Practice

Forgive yourself
for something.

Evening Practice

Forgive someone else
for something.

CRYSTALS FOR
SCORPIO SEASON

INTIMACY

Red Tourmaline   Scorpio season propels you to create
warmth and closeness. But opening yourself up to the
vulnerability of intimacy demands courage. Whether you are
setting the stage for sexual intimacy or emotional intimacy,
Red Tourmaline will help you feel confident enough to
embrace deep connection with others. Other crystals for
intimacy are Garnet, Shiva Lingam or Red Aventurine.

TRANSFORMATION

Moldavite   Transformation brings both endings and
new beginnings. Moldavite will help you spiritually and
emotionally adjust when change comes into your life – when
a relationship has run its course, a shift is needed in the
work arena or a new adventure calls your name. When the
transformation you are undergoing is more subtle in texture,
like saying goodbye to an old habit, Moldavite will help you
align with your new reality. Or try Shungite, Moss Agate
or Tugtupite.

FORGIVENESS

Dioptase   Whether you need to be kinder to yourself or let go
of hurt that someone else has caused you, forgiveness doesn't
happen all at once. It's a process that you set in motion. Finding
forgiveness requires self-love, self-worth and understanding.
Dioptase can help you practice forgiveness by supporting you
with its gentle and loving vibrations. You could also turn to
Black Moonstone, Rhodochrosite or Pink Tourmaline.

WISDOM
AND FREEDOM

Sagittarius season is represented by the archer who shoots high and blazes a trail into new territory. The archer is also a centaur – half horse and half human, half wild and half philosophical. Sagittarius season is a time to feel fiercely alive and simultaneously inspired to ask big, existential questions. It's a season for expanding your boundaries and traveling physically and mentally to understand more about the world and the human experience.

SAGITTARIUS HOROSCOPE
FOR SAGITTARIUS SEASON

You light up the room with your enthusiasm and excitement! The Sun is moving through your area of identity and personality, so it's time to put yourself out there. Enjoy socializing, meeting new people and being out in public. This is a wonderful time to pay attention to how you want to present yourself in the world. Enjoy being yourself.

Morning Practice	Evening Practice
Go for a walk or a jog out in nature.	Memorize an inspiring quote.

CRYSTALS FOR SAGITTARIUS SEASON

INNER WISDOM

Azurite   In Sagittarius season, the archer knows that the best way to take aim is to trust your inner wisdom. When you are connected to your true self, it's easier to make choices. Life feels more satisfying. Azurite is the stone to hold and carry when you want to bolster your self-confidence and tune into your wisdom. Or choose Idocrase, Shattuckite or Amethyst.

EXPANSION

Jasper   Ruled by the gas giant Jupiter, Sagittarius is the sign of expansion. During this season, you can move beyond anything that is limiting you. Is there an area of your life in which you feel trapped in a cage? Maybe if you take a closer look, you'll find that the door to the cage has been open the entire time. Feel the freedom and expansion that is available to you with the help of Jasper. This enlivening stone will help you break out into new territory. Alternatives are Blue Topaz, Pink Chalcedony or Ruby Iolite.

ADVENTURE AND TRAVEL

Turquoise   When you're setting out in search of new horizons, reach for Turquoise as your talisman for protection and luck. Travel and adventure require equal parts bravery and boldness, but the reward is an expanded mindset and perspective. Let Turquoise be your steady support system as you push beyond your boundaries to discover excitement, new opportunity and enlightenment. You could also use Green Opal, Smoky Quartz or Aventurine.

CAREER
AND GOALS

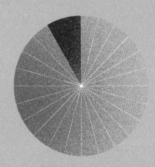

Like the mountain goat, in Capricorn season
you are primed to choose your footing carefully as
you make your ascent. Capricorn season brings practical
and productive forward motion. Use this energy efficiently
and tactically. You may choose to counterbalance this drive
and ambition with a large dose of acceptance, both
of yourself and others. Remember to give yourself a
break; you are trying your best.

SAGITTARIUS HOROSCOPE
FOR CAPRICORN SEASON

With the Sun moving through your
zone of money and self-worth, you have
a chance to get your financial house
in order. Create or refine your budget,
decide if your spending is matching
up with your values and think about
what security means to you. This is the
season to feel grounded and secure.

Affirmation

EVERY DAY, IN EVERY WAY,
I AM GETTING BETTER.

Morning Practice

Write down your goals.

Evening Practice

Reflect on your
accomplishments.

ACHIEVEMENT

Fluorite   Your Capricorn season recommendation supports
you in taking things one step at a time while staying focused
on your big picture goals. Look to Fluorite. Fluorite's unique
vibration can help you concentrate, while energizing you so
that you can keep moving forwards. Or look for support from
Ocean Jasper, Septarian Nodule or Tiger's Eye.

CAREER

Cat's Eye   Capricorn season is a wonderful time to take
stock. While you think about your work life, keep Cat's Eye by
your side. This stone helps you know your strengths, which is
imperative for a fulfilling career. It will help you feel optimistic
and believe in yourself. Cat's Eye's structured energy helps
you know your personal boundaries and make smart money
choices. You could also use Andradite Garnet, Apatite or
Hawk's Eye.

FOR SELF-ACCEPTANCE

Blue Aragonite   Let calming Blue Aragonite guide you
when you need to feel the soothing balm of self-acceptance.
Capricorn season pushes you to achieve, which may cause
you to question your progress in life. Counterbalance that by
learning to accept yourself for who you are. Blue Aragonite
has a compassionate energy that may inspire you to be less
judgemental towards yourself and show yourself more kindness.
Other crystals for self-acceptance are Prasiolite, Amethyst
or Shungite.

FRIENDSHIP AND VISION

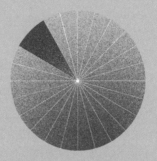

Aquarius season pushes people and ideas to the forefront. What are your big ideas for the future? And who is in your community? Your vision for the future may also be a vision for humanity. Take the time to research causes to which you might contribute time, money and resources. Your friends, communities and social groups are extra important during this season, so prioritize the people who mean the most to you.

SAGITTARIUS HOROSCOPE FOR AQUARIUS SEASON

Sagittarius, find your voice during Aquarius season. The Sun is transiting your zone of communication and community. It's a wonderful time to write, talk and connect with others. You may also find opportunities to think about things in a new way. Make way for fresh ideas and mental breakthroughs.

Affirmation

I LIVE IN THE MOMENT WITH
HIGH HOPES FOR THE FUTURE.

Morning Practice

eate a vision board and make it the
st thing you see when you wake up.

Evening Practice

Call a friend for a
meaningful chat.

CRYSTALS FOR
AQUARIUS SEASON

FRIENDSHIP

Bismuth   Aquarius season asks you to turn towards your
community. What can you offer? What will you receive?
Friends enrich your life in so many ways, but mostly by
encouraging your feeling of belonging – a natural mood
booster. Bismuth has an expansive energy that helps you join
with others in a shared sense of community. Carry Bismuth as a
reminder that you are connected to others. Or you could reach
for Carnelian, Sunset Sodalite or Blue Apatite.

FAITH IN THE FUTURE

Cavansite   The future is uncertain. Sometimes you need a
boost to help you trust in the potential and possibility of what
the future can become. In that case, reach for Cavansite.
This stone has a sweet vibe of positivity that can give you the
courage to believe in your biggest dreams for the future. Some
alternatives are Peridot, Muscovite or Auralite 23.

VIBRATIONAL LIFT

Apophyllite   When Aquarius season asks you to turn
your attention to what is possible, it helps to have a positive
outlook. Without suppressing any challenging feelings (those
are important and need to be processed), pay some special
attention to the positive things in your life and work to create
an enduring, positive mindset. If you need a little extra support,
reach for Clear or Green Apophyllite. This high-vibe crystal
can lift your spirits and help you feel full of potential. You
could also try Quartz, Hematite or Angelite.

INTUITION AND SPIRITUALITY

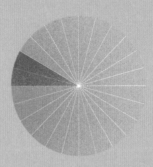

The most mystical season of all, Pisces season is the time to tune into your intuition. Slide like a slippery fish into the sphere of your dreams, faith, spirituality, compassion and creativity. This is a moment to rest, reflect and look inwards. Reconnect with your imagination. Feel your feelings. Plug into your spirituality or whatever makes you feel connected to the universe.

SAGITTARIUS HOROSCOPE FOR PISCES SEASON

The Sun is moving through your area of home, family and emotions. Home is where you feel safe and supported. It's a great time to focus on settling into your space, and making your inner sanctum cosy and comforting. You may find yourself focused on family or those people in your inner circle. Don't be surprised if your emotions are flowing – take the time to tend to your feelings.

Morning Practice

Record your dreams.

Evening Practice

Do some freewriting
to clear your mind.

CRYSTALS FOR
PISCES SEASON

COMPASSION

Lavender Quartz Lavender Quartz helps you feel peace and understanding for others. It will bestow upon you the softness that you need to open up to other people's perspectives. It will also allow you to dissolve drama with a heightened sense of empathy. This soothing and healing stone can offer strength while you stand in someone else's shoes. A compassionate life is a fulfilling life. As an alternative, turn to Thulite, Prehnite with Epidote or Fluorite.

INTUITION

Pink Opal When you trust your inner guidance system you have ultimate clarity. Harness the power of your intuition in Pisces season with the help of Pink Opal. This stone will help you connect to yourself and to your guides. It raises the volume on your inner 'Yes' or 'No' by quietening any distractions and helping you connect within. Other crystals for intuition are Clear Quartz, Moldavite or Dumortierite.

FOR FAITH

Celestite Faith can be thought of as a complete trust or confidence in someone or something. With a little bit of faith you may find it easier to contend with fear or anxiety. But trust and faith must be developed from within. In Pisces season, harness the power of high-vibrational Celestite to help you move beyond unnecessary fears as you put your trust in something bigger. You could also use Vatican Stone, Apophyllite or Turquoise.

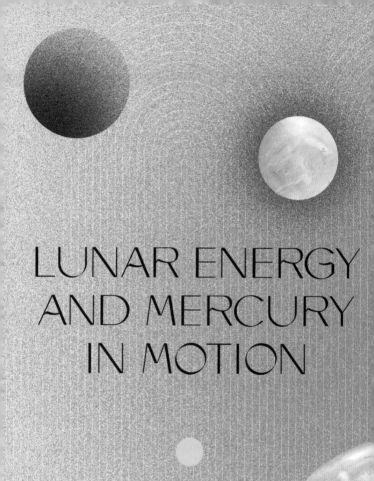

LUNAR ENERGY
AND MERCURY
IN MOTION

THE LUNAR
CYCLE

In astrology, the Moon is a catalyst, helping us to move
forwards with our goals and intentions.

The 29-day lunar cycle begins in darkness. The Moon
then appears as a faint crescent and grows bigger until it's
full. This process, from darkness to Full Moon, mirrors the
incubation and development of your own creative process.
Then, the Moon wanes until it completely disappears,
reflecting another stage of the creative cycle – the process of
releasing your efforts and making space for another cycle to
begin. This allows new thoughts and ideas to emerge.

Each of the eight phases of the Moon cycle offers a
different type of energy, which we will explore in this
chapter. You can follow the Moon through the lunar month
with crystal recommendations, setting your intentions in
alignment with the New Moon and letting the lunar cycle
help you make that intention into reality. The lunar cycle
will also help you cleanse and release so that you can gently
transition into the next phase.

By using crystals to work with the lunar cycle you can
activate the potential of the Moon and amplify its energy.
Through visualization or meditation, tap into the unique
energies of each stage of the Moon cycle with the following
crystals. For the suggested rituals at each phase, choose a
crystal from the recommended options, or substitute with
your favourite crystal.

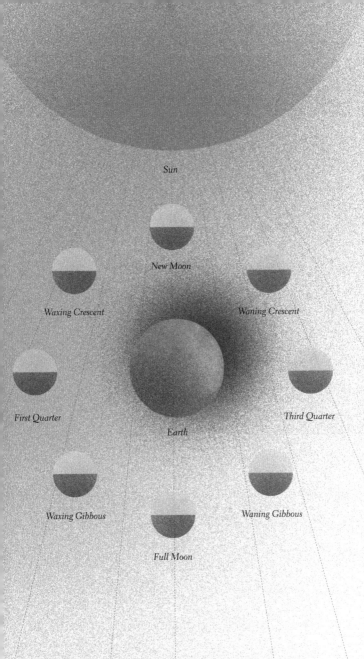

SET YOUR NEW INTENTIONS

The Moon is dark. This is a time for reflection and a time to connect with your inner self. Use your energy to envision what you would like to make happen. What do you desire? What are your dreams? Anything is possible – imagine that you are planting seeds of intention that will manifest and grow throughout the Waxing Moon Phase. The New Moon is a quiet and emotional time and you may discover that, as you think about what you would like to create, many different feelings arise. Excitement, anticipation, fear, worry – whatever feelings arise, make space for those feelings and be gentle with yourself. Listen to your intuition and imagine your next steps.

Black Moonstone can support you during the delicate and sensitive New Moon vibration. It offers wellsprings of patience and peace as you work with your emotions and reflect on your life. When your dreams are germinating under the surface, Black Moonstone can help you trust your own process.

Labradorite opens your third eye wide so that you can tune into your intuition and design your goals in accordance with your path and purpose.

Pink Sapphire's loving energy can buffer you and help you feel emotionally at ease.

Ametrine provides sweet joy and concentrated focus so that you can set intentions with confidence.

TRUST,
INSPIRATION, SERENITY
AND DELIGHT

New Moon Ritual

Freewrite about what you yearn for and anything else that's on your mind. Then jot down your intentions for this Moon cycle on a piece of paper and place your chosen crystal on top.

NURTURE YOUR INTENTIONS

Your seeds of intention are germinating under the soil, and maybe some of the plants are just beginning to sprout. As the lunar energy builds momentum, make sure that you have the resources you need to achieve your goals. Provide structure and support for yourself. This cycle is just beginning to take shape, so consider how your choices will determine your direction – maybe there are changes you'd like to make to your goals. Remain curious throughout this process, because anything is possible!

Turquoise is a powerhouse of a crystal that can deftly carry you through the precarious Waxing Crescent phase. At this moment you need a subtle combination of confidence, discernment, curiosity and commitment. Turquoise can help you understand the truth of what you need to create, and it can help you stay open and accepting of your process. Use this stone as you decide what you really want to manifest and commit to during this Moon cycle.

Shattuckite helps you intuitively illuminate your path so that you can make the decisions that are right for you.

Pyrite offers crystalline protection and is a wonderful choice to help you realize your goals.

Orange Calcite gives you mental focus and lots of energy for the journey ahead.

TRUTH, INTUITION, MANIFESTATION AND FOCUS

Waxing Crescent Moon Ritual

Read and rewrite your intentions for this Moon cycle.
Decorate the paper and place your chosen crystal back on top.

BUILD YOUR MOMENTUM

Look around your garden of intentions and discover what is growing. Have your goals started to take shape? If so, how are they coming along? Do you need more support? Perhaps you have had surprising results? At the First Quarter Moon the constraints of reality can be intimidating. You have big dreams, but sometimes you encounter resistance when dreams make contact with real world limitations. Maybe there is more work required than you had foreseen, or there are real-world issues with time, money, support or other resources. Give yourself lots of encouragement. Pivot, and reassess if necessary. This is an exciting, high energy time, so keep taking action and building momentum.

Bumblebee Jasper When reality, and all of its limitations, hits, Bumblebee Jasper can help you stay the course with confidence. Lean on this crystal when you need the energy to just keep moving forwards. It will subdue your fears and inspire you to push past your comfort zone.

Peridot is a cheery companion that will help you look at any situation with optimism.

Tangerine Quartz offers creative potential that makes problem solving effortless.

Aventurine will vitalize you and give you the confidence to keep going.

CONFIDENCE,
OPTIMISM, CREATIVITY AND
VITALITY

First Quarter Moon Ritual

Light a candle, hold your chosen crystal and
visualize your intentions being realized.

DEVELOP YOUR INTENTIONS

It's astonishing what a little effort can create! Now that you've made it to the Waxing Gibbous phase of the Moon cycle, you are starting to see the effects of the intentions that you set. If your goal was to improve your nutrition, you may be feeling better already. If you felt motivated to get out there and start eating, you may have started some new conversations. Whatever the last few days have revealed, now is the time to roll up your sleeves and actively give shape to your garden. What will you weed out? What is working, and what isn't working? What changes might you make? The intensity has almost peaked to take tender care of your emotional well-being as you keep putting in effort towards your dreams.

Jet Jet's grounding energy will help you establish deep root systems for your developing intentions. When you need strength and motivation to keep pushing forwards with your goals, this stone will support you. As a bonus, jet has a sheltering vibration that can steady you emotionally and help you surge forwards with optimism and hope.

Hematite offers balance and protection, helping you proactively take care of yourself during this active time.

Carnelian lights your fire with sparkling enthusiasm and convinces you to tune into your creative side.

Blue Lace Agate calms your mind, allowing you to weed through your options and make solid decisions.

GROUNDING,
PROTECTION, ENTHUSIASM
AND PEACE OF MIND

Waxing Gibbous Moon Ritual

While holding or wearing your chosen crystal, do something that feels active or expressive, such as dancing, painting, gardening, cooking or singing. Imagine your goals and repeat your intentions.

HARVEST

Everything is revealed under the light of the Moon. The attempts you've made, your wins, your losses. It's time to get out in the garden and harvest the crop. Regardless of whether the bounty lives up to your expectations, there is something to appreciate and celebrate. At the Full Moon, honour what you've created and give gratitude to yourself for your commitment. This phase represents the push and pull of two opposite energies as the Moon is in the opposite sign to the Sun. The result is a highly polarized and intense energy that can heighten emotions, pull you in two different directions, or cause you to realize something important. Make sure to be very gentle with yourself and those around you.

White Moonstone symbolizes the Full Moon and all of its glorious creativity and excitement. This pearly white crystal shines a bright light so that you can see clearly. As you examine the fruits that you've cultivated during the Waxing Moon phase, use the receptive and healing energy of White Moonstone to help you accept and celebrate. It's time for gratitude, and this comforting crystal will help you open up to that feeling.

Green Apatite is an antidote to the drama of the Full Moon – use it to highlight joy and abundance.

Jade has a subtle, soothing energy that imparts an optimistic attitude.

Stilbite connects the heart, mind and intuition – this can help you rationally balance your emotions while still opening up to divine insight.

EMOTIONAL EXPLORATION, ABUNDANCE, PEACEFULNESS AND RECEPTIVITY

Full Moon Ritual

Hold your chosen crystal and write down three things that you are grateful for. The Full Moon is also a great time to cleanse your crystals. Place them outside or on a windowsill and let them bathe in the Moon's healing energy.

REFLECT AND REVIEW

Now that the intensity of the full reveal has begun to wane, you can settle deeper into your new reality. Indulge yourself and enjoy. As the Moon has moved through waxing to waning, this is the beginning of a less active and more receptive phase. This means that you can simply sit with the ebbing fullness of what is. Begin a process of compassionate review. What have you learned? What will you do differently in the next Moon cycle? Each lunar cycle reveals an older, more experienced version of who you are becoming. So sink into this moment of reflection and get to know yourself once more.

Obsidian offers a protective energy that buffers and supports. Use it at the Waning Gibbous phase of the Moon cycle to release the past and securely recline into the experience of the moment. Obsidian's cleansing vibes can help you remove any junk from your thought patterns, allowing you to think from a new perspective. Harness its clarifying energy to appraise your situation with equanimity and objectivity.

Tiger's Eye is for encouragement and strength as you review your progress and make plans for improvement.

Citrine offers joy and optimism so that you can look at your accomplishments through a positive lens.

Celestite provides tranquillity as you come down off the high of the Full Moon.

PROTECTION,
STRENGTH, JOY AND
TRANQUILLITY

Waning Gibbous Moon Ritual

Pour yourself some tea, water, or other drink of your choice, and take the time to sit and quietly appreciate the moment. With your chosen crystal nearby, review your intention and gratitude lists.

Get comfortable letting go so that you can make space for new things. At the Last Quarter Moon allow the leaves to fall and the fading plants to return to the soil. A tree drops its leaves to conserve resources. Take stock of what you want to let go of, so that you can use your energy wisely. Is there someone you need to forgive? Do you need to release your expectations and accept something about your life? Release the past or an outdated way of thinking, let go and forgive. Maybe you declutter your closet, acknowledge your reality, admit your mistakes, get really honest with yourself, or forgive yourself or others. The Last Quarter Moon asks that you put in a little effort to let go of the emotions and ideas that are taking up excess energy.

LOVE, SUPPORT, GROUNDING AND GENTLE SELF-REFLECTION

Rose Quartz is an emotional balm that can help you forgive yourself and others. As the Last Quarter Moon inspires you to release your expectations and accept your current reality, you need a soothing support that helps you open up compassionately. Rose Quartz brings playful, loving vibes and helps you gently accept a situation and move forwards.

Rutilated Quartz offers a powerful support in following through on your intentions as you review what you've learned and plan for the next phase.

Smoky Quartz provides grounding, protection and assistance in clearing the thoughts and feelings that you are ready to release.

Amethyst is for gently releasing old mental patterns and contemplating new possibilities.

Last Quarter Moon Ritual

Create a peaceful environment and run a bath for yourself. Place a water-safe, non-toxic crystal (such as Quartz or Amethyst) in the bath while you review your intentions from this moon cycle. Repeat these affirmations, 'I make space for clarity' and 'I release the past'.

STILLNESS AND REST

The lunar energy is encouraging you to turn inwards and be still. All is quiet in the winter of your metaphorical garden. Embracing stillness offers many benefits. By allowing your inner landscape to exist without judgement, you honour who you are now. Slowing down can also help you uncover your values and emotional truth – which may not be so apparent when you are busily running around. And last but not least, rest and quiet will help you recharge your energy for the next cycle. Challenge yourself to slow down and be present in the moment. There will be ample time for new plans and dreams when the next cycle begins.

Serpentine can help you open a gateway to the stillness within and to the profound interconnectedness of the universe. Using this crystal during your Waning Crescent Moon meditations will help you feel buffered and supported in the understanding that there is no-one you need to be and nothing you need to do. Float along with the waves of existence. You'll know when the time is right again for action.

Selenite radiates cleansing energy that can help you release the past cycle and prepare to make a fresh start.

Howlite soothes your spirit and quietens any absurd complaints from your 'inner critic'.

Aquamarine helps you create a meditative state of mind so that you can listen to the stillness within.

CONNECTION WITH
NATURE, CLEANSING,
SOOTHING AND REFLECTION

Waning Crescent Moon Ritual

Sit quietly in the meditation of your choosing. Hold your crystal or place it nearby.

MERCURY
RETROGRADE

Mercury Retrograde deserves attention as it's a chance to review your plans and goals. It's notoriously known for causing technology and communication issues, but the upside of this time period is that it offers an invitation to slow down and re-assess where you are and where you want to go.

Fast-moving Mercury symbolizes connection, communication and technology. Mercury is the part of you that learns, thinks, teaches and talks.

Mercury orbits the Sun about four times as fast as the Earth and every time that Mercury zips past the Earth an optical illusion occurs that makes it look as though Mercury is moving backwards. When Mercury appears to be moving backwards (Mercury Retrograde), it's a great opportunity to slow down. Go back over your thoughts and decisions of recent months and review them. Turn inwards to gain guidance from your intuition.

Mercury Retrograde happens about three times a year and lasts for about three weeks each time. You can use these retrograde periods as a moment to check in with yourself and review your practices, thoughts and relationships. Have you been putting off an uncomfortable conversation? Is there something that you need to be honest about with yourself when it comes to relationships, work or money? What has your body been trying to tell you? Is there some new way that you could step out of your comfort zone? What would help you feel more secure and supported?

Underlying issues tend to rise to the surface during Mercury Retrograde. It's typically advised to make sure that you are extra clear in your communications during these periods, and that you wait until the retrograde period has ended before beginning new projects or signing contracts. But it's an excellent time to pick up where you left off on something – to rethink, redo and review.

YOUR CRYSTAL PRACTICE DURING MERCURY RETROGRADE

Crystal energy can help you slow down your busy mind and tune into your intuition during Mercury Retrograde. As you rethink and review, these crystals will amplify your intuition and clarity.

KEEN INSIGHT

Pietersite   Employ this speckled Quartz for illuminated insight paired with steady determination.

CLARITY AND COMMUNICATION

Aquamarine   This stone soothes and calms the mind while simultaneously boosting your ability to communicate clearly.

CREATIVE THOUGHT

Citrine   A crystal that spurs your imagination, helping you conceptualize how you might like patterns or situations to change.

Beginning of Mercury Retrograde Ritual	End of Mercury Retrograde Ritual
Perform a full and gentle review of the issues most affecting you by writing a journal entry using the following prompt: 'What do I need to see that I'm not seeing when it comes to my …' Give yourself lots of gratitude in the process and call on your chosen crystal to provide understanding and clarity. When you've finished, write down three takeaways on a small piece of paper and place your crystal on top of it for the remainder of the Retrograde. Drawing on the power of your crystal, let your subconscious mind continue to explore and reveal the subtleties of these thoughts and questions over the coming weeks.	Near the end of the Retrograde cycle, set an intention to integrate what you've learned during the past days and weeks. Begin by returning to your piece of paper and your crystal. What came up for you during Mercury Retrograde? Was there a new realization, attitude or interest that emerged? Think about what you may have realized and journal about what you'd like to bring into your life now. Is there an intention (see page 22) or affirmation that could come from this exploration? If so, write it down. Look in a mirror and repeat your intention or affirmation five times while holding your crystal. Remember to thank your crystal and to thank yourself for showing up. For the next two weeks, repeat this daily ritual.

CONCLUSION

This book has taken you deep below the Earth's surface, through the metaphorical caverns of crystals and their symbolism. You've connected the dots of the solar system and the meaning of the astrology you were born with. By pairing the forces of the stars above with the crystals below, you've gained tools that can help you navigate your unique journey with wisdom.

In Part Two, you learned about the crystals that can support your unique astrology. This section included insights for Sagittarius Sun, Moon and Rising signs, along with supportive crystal recommendations for what your sign needs in five key life areas.

Life is always changing and so in Part Three you learned to follow the energy of the Sun as it moves on its annual journey through the zodiac, finding crystals that may help you elaborate on the theme of each astrological season.

Revolving and evolving with changing astrological cycles continued in Part Four, where you paired crystal energy with the ebb and flow of the Moon, and learned to harness the power of crystals in tandem with Mercury Retrograde to perform a trimonthly check-in.

All the answers are already within you. When you choose a crystal, you awaken the vibration of that crystal within yourself. Harness your astro-crystal practice to help you see what already exists inside of you. You have everything you need.

With the cosmos above and the crystals below, you are always connected and supported. Let the stones and the stars strengthen your self-awareness and self-trust as you continue your crystalline cosmic journey.

Crystals and astrology are not intended to be a substitute for medical advice, diagnosis or treatment. Always seek the advice of your qualified healthcare provider.

RESOURCES

GET YOUR BIRTH CHART	www.sandysitron.com/crystals
ASTROLOGY READING	www.sandysitron.com
CRYSTALS	*101 Power Crystals: The Ultimate Guide to Magical Crystals, Gems, and Stones for Healing and Transformation* Judy Hall
CRYSTAL ENERGY HEALING	https://www.kalisaaugustine.com/
SOURCING CRYSTALS RESPONSIBLY	moonrisecrystals.com/
SPIRAL CRYSTALS	spiralcrystals.com/
HOOF AND PAW	hoofandpawuk.com/
ASTROLOGY	*Astrology for Yourself* Demetra George and Douglas Bloch
AFFIRMATION WORK	Transformational coach Dana Balicki: https://danabalicki.com/
AFFIRMATION WORK	*Empowerment: The Art of Creating Your Life as You Want It* Gail Straub and David Gershon
ASTROLOGY EDUCATION	www.thestrology.com
	Ritual Enchantments *A Modern Witch's Guide to Self-Possession* Mya Spalter

FEATURED CRYSTALS

LAURENCE KING

First published in Great Britain in 2022 by Laurence King
an imprint of The Orion Publishing Group Ltd
Carmelite House, 50 Victoria Embankment
London EC4Y 0DZ

An Hachette UK Company

10 9 8 7 6 5 4 3 2 1

A CIP catalogue record for this book is
available from the British Library.

ISBN 978-0-8578-2930-6

Design: Therese Vandling

Printed in China by C&C Offset Printing Co. Ltd

Laurence King Publishing is committed to ethical and
sustainable production. We are proud participants in the
Book Chain Project®. [bookchainproject.com]

BOOK
CHAIN
PROJECT

www.laurenceking.com
www.orionbooks.co.uk